# WHEN INFERTILITY STRIKES

EMMANUEL OKELLO

ISBN 979-888569180-2

# Contents

# CHAPTER ONE

*A GUIDE FOR INFERTILITY REMEDIES* **[1]- Infertility Issues For Women and Men** *Definition of Infertility Infertility as defined by the experts may surprise you. According to guidelines established by infertility specialists, you're not considered to be infertile until you've been trying to get pregnant for one year, if you're under age 35. That means that trying to get pregnant last week and not having signs of pregnancy this week does not mean that you're infertile. What Causes Infertility? Infertility has many causes, and figuring out which applies to you may be very simple - or very difficult. Although women used to bear the brunt of blame for infertility, the truth is that male and female factors share equally in infertility. Consider the following statistics: • One third of infertility is caused by female factors • One third of infertility is caused by male factors • Around 20 percent of infertility is unexplained • Around 10 to 15 percent of infertility is caused by a combination of male and female factors Approximately 20% of couples struggle with infertility at any given time. Infertility has increased as a problem over*

*the last 30 years. Some studies blame this increase on social phenomena, including the tendency for marriage and starting a family to occur at a later age. For women, fertility decreases with increasing age: • married women ages 16-20 = 4.5%. • married women ages 35-40 = 31.8%. • married women over the age of 40 = 70%. Among women, the main causes of infertility are: • Ovulatory disorders - no ovulation or irregular ovulation • Tubal disorders - blocked or infected tubes • Uterine issues - fibroids, polyps or adhesions For men the most common causes of infertility are: • Low sperm count • Decreased sperm motility • Abnormally shaped sperm • No sperm at all in the ejaculate Defining Secondary Infertility Secondary infertility is defined as the condition where a woman is unable to get pregnant or carry a pregnancy to term after already having had one or more children. Some experts put the added caveat of "after 12 months of trying to conceive naturally on their own", to better qualify the term. Some experts define it as occurring anytime after a previous conception, whether that conception ended in a birth or a miscarriage. Some women with endometriosis-associated infertility are not able to become pregnant a second time. Secondary infertility can occur whether the first conception was difficult or easy. It can be due to female issues, male issues, or a combination of both. The costs of treatment Infertility treatments can be difficult enough. Like everything, infertility* *costs vary and can depend on where you live, which physician/practice you see and most importantly, whether your treatment is small, medium, or large. When you're starting out, expect to pay $10 to $15 for an ovulation predictor kit and about the same for home pregnancy kits. A basal body thermometer will run you about $10 to $20. This is the easy stuff. But, for now, let's take it one step at a time.*

# CHAPTER TWO

***[2]-Treatment For Infertility For Men And Women*** *Conceiving a baby is not as easy as it sounds for some couples and there are many reasons why a couple may have trouble getting pregnant. There can be an individual problem with either the man or the woman or it may be that both of them have underlying health issues that combine to have a negative impact on their fertility as a couple. In general men are responsible for about a third of infertility in couples and women a little less than a half. Situations involving individual infertility issues with both the man and the woman can combine to contribute to an overall remaining percentage. Although fertility tends to be considered by most to be a woman's problem, anyone who is dealing with this dilemma should know that it can also be an issue with the male's reproductive system. Causes and Resolutions of Infertility in Men It may be that a blockage prevents sperm from being introduced into ejaculate fluid or a situation that creates higher temperatures in the man's testes could affect sperm production and quality. The average course of treatment for the*

*infertility problem of a blockage of almost any type is to have surgery. These types of surgeries are considered to be of low risk while having a very high rate of success. Fertility drugs to increase their female partner's egg production can also be an option when there is a low sperm count or a low quality level regarding the sperm but realise there will be side effects experienced by the woman who is the one actually taking the medication. When it comes to a situation of 'Sperm Viability' which basically means how alive and active the sperm are, the idea of 'Boxers Vs Briefs' should be taken seriously. Wearing boxers will not have the testicles pressed against the body where they will absorb body heat but instead they have room for air to circulate around them and this will reduce their temperature and that slight reduction in heat can actually make a difference. Causes and Resolutions of Infertility in Women There are many different types and causes of infertility in women that would prevent them from being able to get pregnant or maintain a healthy pregnancy. Endometriosis is a fairly common infertility problem in women that may require several types of treatment infertility doctors can provide: fertility drugs, exploratory surgeries, IUIs, or artificial insemination. Intrauterine insemination (IUI) is a procedure that consists of placing the sperm inside a woman's uterus to facilitate fertilisation. This fertility treatment does not involve the manipulation of a woman's eggs and therefore is not considered an assisted reproductive technology (ART) procedure. Polycystic Ovarian Syndrome, or PCOS, is another common problem that may cause a woman to have a difficult time getting pregnant. In vitro fertilisation, IUIs, and fertility drugs have been proven to help women with PCOS become pregnant. Although it is rare, sometimes women will have an allergy to sperm which causes soreness during intercourse and the body will discard the sperm. Artificial insemination is the treatment infertility patients receive most often for a sperm allergy. Sometimes There Is No Explanation Many couples find it comforting to be moved from an OB-GYN to a reproductive endocrinologist. Couples often go to this type of specialist hoping for a solution to their infertility problem. Unfortunately, if thorough exams come back with both partners receiving a clean bill of health, there is no treatment infertility patients can receive to fix their situation. Unexplained infertility is a term used for patients who seem to be in perfect health but cannot conceive a child. Treatment For Infertility: One Last Thought The care you receive from an endocrinologist could cost you a a lot of money. Some procedures cost tens of thousands of dollars. Other procedures may be covered by your insurance company. To understand exactly what is covered and what is not covered regarding infertility, please check with your provider.*

# CHAPTER THREE

***[3]-Top Three Natural Fertility Treatments***

*Many people find it difficult to imagine the devastating effects that infertility can have on a woman's psyche. However, when a woman is finding it difficult to conceive, it is not only her mind that one needs to worry about, it is her body as well. Conventional medical treatments for infertility can be down right invasive, not to mention painful, and a lot of the modern drugs are extremely harsh on the body's systems. The good news is that, while conventional treatments are dreadful, natural treatments can be extremely relaxing and pleasurable. Ever since the beginning of time there have been women, and men, who find it difficult to reproduce, and believe it or not even then there were treatments for it. The only difference was that people long ago didn't have our technology, so they had to find techniques that worked naturally. These treatments were so effective that even now, in our technologically advanced society, we call on them for help. One prime example of a natural technique that has definitely stood the test of time is acupuncture.*

• *Acupuncture Acupuncture has been used by traditional Chinese herbalists and healers for centuries, and at its rate of success it will most likely continue to be used for several more centuries to come. The truly great thing about acupuncture is while most other fertility treatments specifically target women, acupuncture has proven effective at increasing a man's fertility as well as a woman's. Acupuncture has been put to the test several times and has nearly always come out as causing significant improvement as a whole. The point of acupuncture is not to cure a disease itself, but to direct positive energy and allow the body to heal itself.* • *Self Fertility Massage. The second extremely effective natural fertility treatment is Self Fertility Massage. Self Fertility Massage is a highly advanced form of therapy that combines several different types of massage that are all focused on very specific fertility issues. For instance, one type of massage included in the therapy is Myofascial release. Myofascial release directly affects the myofascial tissues that have a tendency to bind and create blockages; a common cause of infertility. Self Fertility Massage also includes the use of acupressure, which is basically acupuncture without the needles. The best thing is this therapy can be used as a bonding experience between you and your partner, or performed on yourself, by yourself in a quite relaxing moment. • Therapeutic Abdominal Packs. Finally, the third natural therapy on the top three list is...Therapeutic Abdominal Packs. This completely natural oil has been used for centuries as an external healing agent; the oil is placed on the outside of the skin yet penetrates its healing powers all the way through to the organs. Therapeutic Abdominal packs are commonly used in a variety of fertility conditions such as, ovarian and uterine cysts, blocked tubes, uterine fibroids, endometriosis, and much more. A great way to integrate two of these therapies is by using the therapeutic oil in conjunction with the self fertility massage. The truly amazing thing about natural therapy is it has a way of healing not only your body, but your soul as well. Many of these techniques are thought to be so effective because of the amount of peace an individual can find within themselves during such a relaxing moment. Whether you decide to do one treatment or all three, try and forget everything during your sessions...work, bills, everything. Leave all stressful events outside, and just let go for that short period of time. I am sure if you do these things not only will you find yourself far more relaxed, but you may just find yourself pregnant before you know it.*

# CHAPTER FOUR

***[4]-Infertility: Myths and Truths*** *Everyone has their opinion about infertility. If you are unable to conceive and don't know why yet, then you have probably been bombarded with advice and suggestions. Aunties may tell you what home remedies to take and uncles may give you unsolicited advice about intercourse. There are so many myths about infertility yet only a set number of truths. It is your responsibility to find out the truth and to do what is right for you Myth: Infertility is only associated with the female. Truth: Infertility could occur in, either, the male and female. About 40% of cases occur in the female and about 40% occur in the male, whilst 10% is in both partners and 10% is unaccounted for. Myth: If you don't conceive immediately you should see a fertility specialist. Truth: It can take some couples some time to conceive, depending on their circumstances, health issues and contraceptives used. If you're unable to conceive after trying for 12 months, then it is a good idea to see a fertility specialist to run tests on both of you. Myth: Your weight doesn't affect your fertility. Truth: For women,*

*especially, if you are overweight then it could lower your chances of conception. It is a good idea to engage in moderate exercises and eat a balanced diet to lose weight. Myth: It's OK for the man to drink alcohol while trying to conceive. Truth: Alcohol is toxic to sperm because it can play a big role in reducing sperm counts, sexual performance and it can affect the hormones. Myth: Smoking doesn't affect male fertility. Truth: Smoking affects both male and female fertility. It has been linked to low sperm counts as well as low motility in men. Myth: Stress causes infertility. Truth: This is a common misconception that stress causes infertility. So couples are usually told that they must relax or take it easy. Couples are also told that they are too young to worry about it. As a result couples delay consultation with a fertility specialist until they are older. This could lower their chances of conceiving because it is better to seek fertility treatment sooner rather than later. Myth: It's OK to exercise excessively, like bodybuilders do. Truth: Excessive exercise such as body building and weight lifting can affect the production of sperm in men which is the result of heat build-up around the testicles. In women, it can lead to menstrual disorders*

CHAPTER FIVE

***[5]-The 7 Most Common Causes Of Infertility*** *If you have been trying to conceive for more than a year (or six months, if you are (under 30) without success, there is a high probability that you or your partner may be suffering from an infertility issue. It is very important to find out if one of these causes of infertility may be affecting you, because if you know what it is, you can take the right treatment and accelerate your process of getting pregnant, regardless of your age. Explained here, are the 7 most common causes and remedies of infertility: 1- Ovulation Issues This is a condition where a hormonal disorder prevents the normal release of mature eggs from your ovaries each month, which considerably reduces your chances to get pregnant. This condition is called anovulation. To fix it, there are ovulation-stimulating drugs that really help to regulate your ovulation cycle (most well known is called Clomid), but be sure to ask for medical advice before taking it. 2- Damaged eggs When you are in your late 30's or early 40's, the quality of your eggs start declining considerably. This means they*

*are not as "fresh" and start to develop genetic anomalies, which makes it a lot harder to sustain pregnancy. The most recommended action when the causes of infertility are genetic is to find a young egg donor, because you can still develop the baby in your womb with "borrowed" eggs and the probabilities of having a safe pregnancy increases a lot. 3- Endometriosis This condition is recognized by painful menstrual cycles and heavy menstrual bleeding. Endometriosis occurs when part of the endometrial tissue, that is inside your uterus, starts to grow out of it and blocks the fallopian tubes. This is one of the most common causes of infertility and can be solved by a small surgical procedure called Laparoscopy. This surgery is not a particularly pleasing process, but women that do it increase by 40/60% their possibilities to get pregnant 18 months after the surgery. 4- Polycystic Ovaries Syndrome Conceiving with polycystic ovaries is harder than normal but is very achievable. Polycystic Ovaries Syndrome (PCOS) causes a hormonal disorder in your body so you start producing more masculine hormones than feminine ones, interrupting the regularity of your periods. This dramatically reduces your chances to conceive. The most effective way to treat this hormonal disorder is with fertility drugs (the most popular are Clomid and Femara), but you should do it with the supervision of your gynaecologist or a fertility endocrinologist because he must indicate to you the right dosage for it to work. 5- Blocked Fallopian Tubes When the fallopian tubes are blocked, it makes it very hard for your eggs to arrive at the uterus and be in contact with the sperm. There are many causes that could provoke this, such as Chlamydia (a sexually transmitted disease), pelvic inflammatory disease or previous sterilisation surgery. The way to fix this is with Laparoscopy surgery, but if the blockage can't be removed successfully, In Vitro Fertilisation treatment may work. However, keep in mind that it is a really expensive treatment. 6- Sperm Issues The main causes of infertility in males are low sperm count and slow sperm mobility. There are fertility drugs to increase the sperm count and they usually improve their conceiving chances by 25%. Another option to this problem is Artificial Insemination or Intracytoplasmic sperm injection (which means to directly inject the sperm into the egg) 7- Overweight This is by far one of the most common causes of infertility and is easily overlooked. Watch out for your weight, since elevated levels of insulin in your body can mess around with your hormonal balance, complicating the conception and increasing the possibilities of pregnancy complications; like gestational diabetes. Studies have revealed that even a small reduction in your weight (about 5%) can greatly increase your chances to get pregnant if you are having trouble conceiving. So as you see, there are many causes of infertility that could be preventing you from getting pregnant, and the more age you have when you are trying to conceive, the harder it gets.*

# CHAPTER SIX

***[6]-Female Infertility And Its Causes*** *Every woman has a dream to become a mother and to experience those 9 months of pregnancy and weave dreams every day for the baby. Also, to become a mother is considered to be the greatest happiness in a woman's life. But infertility shatters this dream. Not only one or two women but also a major part of female society is struggling with this serious problem. Because of which, becoming a mother's dream becomes very difficult. Infertility has no single cause but it is said that a disease related to women with periods cycle and getting pain during sex may cause of infertility. For a couple, it is the greatest happiness of the world that they should have a happy family. But many couples are bereaved from this happiness due to infertility. Infertility can be defined as a problem of not having children. Also, it refers to a condition in which a woman is unable to conceive. It may occur in both men and women but the problem of not having children is often considered to be female infertility. Substantially, infertility in men, may be the reason for not being pregnant. Female*

*infertility can be understood as an incompetence to conceive or a problem where a woman is unable to get pregnant even after a year or more years of regular unprotected sexual intercourse. This problem may occur in two situations. First, it may happen post marriage and secondly, some women may find difficulty in conceiving a second time after having a child. So, in this way it can be said that infertility may be of two types. In this book, we are going to find out the causes behind female infertility. You may get rid of this serious issue quickly by knowing initial causes of female infertility. It is believed that sooner the treatment, greater the relief. But, first you have to identify the causes listed below. 1. Periods Problem: When a woman has irregular periods, painful periods and absence of periods or no periods then she may have female infertility problems. Some women do not have periods on time while others feel a lot of pain during periods. Both the situations may indicate the risk of infertility. 2. Bleeding from Uterus: Other than periods, lite bleeding from the uterus may also be a cause of sterility. This kind of bleeding is known as fibroids which is a type of tumour and is caused by too much tissue formation in muscles. A woman may conceive even suffering from this problem but the possibility of miscarriage due to this tumor may increase. In most of the cases, it is handled through surgery. 3. Pain during Sex: There should be no pain during sex but if a woman feels pain during sexual intercourse then it's a matter of thinking. In this situation, consult with a specialist immediately and do not to avoid it else this may result as endometriosis. 4. Depression or Insomnia: You may feel symptoms of insomnia during periods of endometriosis and along with this it is also feasible that you have to go through from depression. Analyse these symptoms and find out if it is related to sterility, if yes then you may see your doctor immediately. 5. Sex Hormone Disorder: When the testosterone level increases in the body, it may results as hair growth on the face too especially on the upper lips, chin, chest and abdomen area. In this, the problem of hair thinning on the head can also be seen. Keep in mind that all these symptoms are caused because of a sex hormone disorder i.e. testosterone. 6. Overweight: None of a woman can see herself getting overweight but an imbalance in weight may come due to many reasons. Nevertheless, after change in food intake and doing regular exercise, if weight is not decreased then it can be female sterility. 7. Loss of Sex Desire: Sterility is not directly linked to the lack of mind during sex but there is a connection of both. Lose of sex desire, depression, depression causes stress, getting pain during sex because of endometriosis, If all these happen then these may cause to female infertility.*

# CHAPTER SEVEN

***[7]-Male Infertility Causes*** *Many people think that infertility is only a problem for females. This is totally not the case since about 30% of couples who have problems conceiving are due to the man's infertility. The other 30% is due to the woman's infertility and the remaining 40% is unexplainable but attributed to the combination of many factors regarding both the male and female. Basically, the process of a man's fertility is regarding the production of mature and healthy sperm and depositing the sperm where it can fertilise an egg. There are numerous male infertility causes but these are the most common: Low Sperm Count This is the most common among male infertility causes. Sperm count should normally be above 15 million sperm per millilitre of semen according to the World Health Organisation in 2010; Having lower than this means that the man is infertile and will have a difficult time impregnating a woman. Affected men won't know about this problem until a test is done because there are no symptoms for this condition. Low sperm count can be an adverse effect of smoking because of the toxins in*

*cigarettes. Excessive alcohol consumption can also cause this problem. Failure to Ejaculate A lot of men are infertile because they cannot ejaculate. Some men cannot ejaculate during stressful or demanding situations but can normally ejaculate during other circumstances. However, there are other men who completely cannot ejaculate. The cause is still unknown but most reproductive experts believe that it is only a psychological problem. This problem is not as common as the other male infertility causes. Abnormal Sperm Some men only produce improperly formed sperm. There are some types of abnormal sperm that have very low mobility thus these sperm have a difficult time in reaching the egg. Some sperm are abnormally shaped so that penetrating and fertilising an egg is difficult and almost impossible. The cause of abnormal sperm is usually genetic in nature and is passed from one generation to another but alcohol and drug abuse can also cause this problem. Abnormal sperm is one of the leading male infertility causes. Prolonged High Scrotal Temperature When a man is seated for a long period of time, scrotal temperatures significantly rise and the sperm's mobility is adversely affected. This is the reason why drivers have a harder time conceiving. Tight underwear and pants also cause high scrotal temperature since the testicles are closer to the body. A physiological condition wherein the veins in the scrotum area are enlarged can also raise the scrotal temperature. Blocked Sperm Ducts Some men have sperm ducts that are damaged or totally blocked therefore the sperm is unable to reach the partner's egg. This can be a congenital problem but it can also be caused by infection or trauma in the area. For infection, medication can take care of this but for damage or Congenital blockage surgery is the only option to correct the problem.*

# CHAPTER EIGHT

***[8]-Herbal Treatment Of Male Infertility***

*When there is a sexual activity between a man and a woman for a period of about a year, especially during the period of ovulation and no pregnancy occurs, it is termed infertility. Simply put, infertility is a failure to carry pregnancy, and in most cases, the problem may be difficult to treat. The journey from ovulation to fertilisation and finally into pregnancy is a very intricate process and some things must be in place before pregnancy can occur. Infertility in men is often as a result of low sperm count or other anatomical abnormalities. Exposures to toxins, testicular injuries, alcohol consumption, hormonal disorders etc, are some of the things that can lead to infertility in men. The most common cause of infertility in men is called varicocele, which is a dilated vein of the spermatic cord. For women, when there is a failure in the ovulatory cycle, like blocked fallopian tube, or uterine fibroids, it leads to infertility. Stress or fears of parenthood are some psychological issues that may contribute to infertility in women. There has been, of late, the discovery of proven herbal and nutritional approaches to the treatment of infertility and low sperm count. Men who are diabetic are more susceptible to infertility, especially when it is not properly treated. Also, men with multiple sexual partners are prone to contact sexually transmitted diseases like gonorrhea, syphilis or Chlamydia, and these diseases can lead to low sperm count. Malnutrition in men leads to either underweight or overweight; deficiency of zinc vitamins and amino acids, and these are chemicals that are vital to the building of sperm and the absence of these leads to low sperm count. Excess alcohol intake, smoking of cigarettes or heroin, cocaine and the use of bodybuilding steroids in men reduces sperm count. Working under severe stressful conditions, especially when the work requires sitting down all day, Working in an overheated environment or driving long distances with overheated vehicles reduces sperm count in men. All this goes to show that men are more susceptible to infertility than women. Prevention of low sperm count In order to prevent low sperm count, it is important to run away from health damaging habits, like having multiple sexual partners, smoking of cigarettes or cocaine and marijuana, alcohol intake etc. Also all habits that lead to chronic stress should be avoided. All junk food, like stimulants e.g. coffee, strong tea and other unwholesome food should be avoided. Very hot baths, saunas, exposing the testis to a very hot environment raises the temperature of the testicles and must be avoided in order to run away from low sperm count. Treatment: As much as it is known that infertility in men can occur as a result of many factors, it is gratifying to note that several herbal nutritional supplements have been used over the years and the results are encouraging. Where some "high tech medications" have failed, herbal medicines have restored life and joy to many men. Nutrients like zinc are required, selenium, vitamin A,C,E and B complex, amino acids, essential fatty acids etc are necessary ingredients needed to make sperm healthy and maintain a high motility and energy . This must be in place before conception can take place. And all the above nutrients are best when they are sourced naturally. Nutrition plays a vital role in the treatment of male infertility and low sperm count. E.g., carrots, potatoes, onions and garlic are good sources of zinc. Fish, liver, vegetables like garden egg, cucumber etc, provide vitamin and zinc. Substances like B-carotene and lycopene improve sperm motility. Lycopene is responsible for the red colours of tomatoes. B-carotene is produced from carotene. Some nutritional supplements which contain a reasonable amount of antioxidants are equally very helpful in restoring men's fertility.*

# CHAPTER NINE

***[9]-Ayurvedic Treatment for Infertility in Females*** *It is often believed that ovulatory disorders are the most common reasons for difficulty faced by women in conceiving. 30% of female infertility cases happen on account of ovulatory disorders. Common problems pertaining to ovulation are hormonal problems like inability to produce normal follicles which, in turn, causes failure of producing mature eggs, malfunctioning of the hypothalamus, and malfunctioning of the pituitary glands. Unruptured follicle syndrome, scarred ovaries, and premature menopause are other causes of poor ovulation. Turning to natural fertility cure with ayurvedic treatment for ovulation is a potential way of therapeutic healing from infertility issues. Ayurvedic View on Female Infertility Amidst, the mad rush of the modern lifestyle conceiving has become a major problem among majority couples. Besides seeking conventional treatment it is very important to resort to alternative courses of treatment like ayurvedic treatment for pregnancy. Ayurveda regards the lack of nutrition in the reproductive tissue; Shukra*

*Dhatu as the prime reason for infertility in women. This mainly happens on account of the presence of toxins in the body and poor digestion. Some other causes of infertility are anxiety, depression, insomnia etc. Ayurvedic doctors often prescribe the use of dried banyan tree bark powder mixed with sugar to treat infertility issues; this is a trusted solution for ayurvedic medicine for blocked fallopian tubes. Improved Fertility with Ayurvedic Treatment for Blocked Fallopian Tubes 20% of infertility cases in women occur on account of the blocked fallopian tube problem. An obstruction in the fallopian tube hinders the egg from travelling down to the tube. It also prevents the sperm from reaching out to the egg which causes problems in fertilisation. In order to reduce inflammation in the fallopian tube and promote blood circulation, resort to herbs. The following herbs are ideal for facilitating Ayurvedic treatment for blocked fallopian tubes- ginseng, goldenseal, dong quai, red clover, chamomile, calendula etc. These herbs can kill any form of bacteria, like yeast which prevents fertility. Dong Quai capsule is a vital ayurvedic medicine for blocked fallopian tubes. It effectively reduces tissue congestion, muscle cramps, and improves circulation to the reproductive organs. Consider taking a fertility massage. It helps in breaking up scar tissues and improves blood circulation around the tubes. Massaging almond, lavender, or olive oil over the pubic bone is an effective natural cure. Conceive naturally with ayurvedic Treatment for Pregnancy Pregnancy and childbirth is undeniably the most rejuvenating experience in the life of a woman. Most ayurvedic medicine for blocked fallopian tubes contains herb components. Ayurveda aims at keeping the body healthy through the use of natural remedies by regulating ayurvedic treatment for ovulation. Herbs like Stinging nettle nourishes the uterus and strengthens the kidney and adrenal gland, Black cohosh is an antispasmodic which reduces period cramps and stimulates the ovaries. The herb Vitex-Agnus Cactus increases the progesterone level and regulates anovulation, amenorrhea, and premenstrual stress. Wild Yam is generally considered to be one of the best fertility herbs for twins and it largely boosts the progesterone count in women. Herbs effectively regulate the hormone and nourish the body in order to conceive better. Combat Pregnancy Issues with Ayurvedic Treatment for Infertility In Females Besides ovulation disorder, other factors causing infertility in women are as follows- uterine fibroids, endocrine disorders, and anatomical defects in the uterus. Some vital herbs facilitating ayurvedic treatment for pregnancy are as follows- • Shatavari-Asparagusracemosus or Shatavari is a spinous under-shrub which bears numerous tuberous roots. This herb is often used to nourish the ovum and increase fertility. • Lodhra- This is an evergreen tree which increases the level of follicular stimulating hormone and luteinizing hormone. It also has several anti-inflammatory properties. • Ashoka- This too is a small evergreen tree, the bark of this tree bears a stimulating effect on the endometrium and ovarian tissue. Ashoka is a power herb for ayurvedic treatment for ovulation. • Kumari- Also known as Aloe barbadensis is a short-stem perennial plant. The consumption of this herb leads to the in-vitro production of oestradiol and progesterone. Power of Ayurveda in Curing Infertility Ayurveda as a form of alternative cure dates back to over several thousand years even before modern medicine existed. Ayurveda specialists aim at healing the whole body naturally without any medical interference. Some quick tips are as follows- • Enhance the presence of Shukra Dhatu in the body with foods like pineapple which is healthy for ovum. Consuming quinoa also increases estrogenic activity in the body. • Make use of the medicated oil basti via the rectum. It eliminates the doshas from the rectum and improves ovum quality. • Shirodhara therapy is a special rhythmic movement of the medicated oils on the forehead. It stimulates the hypothalamus and pituitary glands which leads to adequate hormone secretion. • Phala Gritam is a great ayurvedic medicine which helps treat female infertility. When consumed with milk in the form of liquefied butter it cures functional problems pertaining to conceiving. Be it ayurvedic treatment for blocked fallopian tubes or ayurvedic treatment for infertility in the female, Ayurveda aims at adopting a holistic approach towards a cure. Ayurvedic medicines essentially have their roots in herbs and natural substances which serve as an alternate source of cure bearing no- critical side-effects on the body.*

# CHAPTER TEN

***[10]-Approaching Fertility Issues in a Holistic Manner*** *In this day and age, fertility and infertility issues are not as difficult to deal with as they were in the past. Science has made advances, which have allowed people to take a closer look and understand the complexities of the human reproductive system - including how non-health related factors affect the body's performance. Conceiving a child, more than just requiring top physical health, also requires that a couple be on a stable level emotionally. There are problems and needs in the relationship that must be addressed. This is where the holistic approach comes in. Fertility issues, when approached with a combination of complementary and conventional care works therapy, become no-brainers. In using the holistic approach, it is important for couples to have a working understanding of how their bodies actually work. For females, they are born with an estimated 2 million egg cells. Hormones released by the pituitary gland stimulate ovulation and development of these egg cells. Oestrogen and progesterone prepare the lining of the uterus and cervix for*

*conception while the vagina discharges cervical mucus prior to ovulation. Males, on the other hand, produce millions of sperm throughout their lifetime, beginning with puberty. The semen ejaculated during intercourse is a mixture of the sperm cells and secretions from the prostate. The sperm reaches the egg cells through the cervix, uterus and up to the fallopian tube before the fertilised egg finally implants itself in the uterus lining. While the process of conceiving, as mentioned above, is quite technical and scientific, it must be remembered that sexual intercourse at the time of ovulation still is not enough. The pressure of having sex with conception in mind can have a negative effect on orgasm and ejaculation, which could result in lesser chances of fertilization, as both are intended to facilitate the meeting of the egg and the sperm. Examples of holistic complementary treatments that can aid in improving fertility are acupuncture, Chinese herbal medicine, reflexology, homoeopathy, creative healing, meditation, visualisation, aromatherapy and massage, shiatsu, Indian Ayurvedic herbs, yoga, and the Jeyarani fertility program. These can be partnered with many forms of conventional medicine. Diagnosis and investigation is important as it can lower the chances of requiring actual invasive testing. There are also ultrasound scans that can comfortably test the timing of ovulation, as well as the uterus' condition for future implantation. Pelvic anatomy tests and infection screens can also be done, to determine whether there are any diseases that may get in the way of healthy fertilisation. It may also be convenient to do a hormone output test on a woman and sperm analysis for the man. This is because when a certain test is done and they have seen the problem, there will be a proper treatment to address infertility. Because complementary therapies alter the balance and flow of body energy, they can solve problems of infertility, which the aforementioned medical tests cannot anticipate or reach. This combination holistic approach, then, can solve not only infertility issues but improve overall health and decrease general stress. Of course, having proper exercise and a great eating habit can also help address infertility issues. This is because obese or overweight people will have a hard time conceiving*

# CHAPTER ELEVEN

***[11]-Three Important Principles Behind Holistic Medicine*** *Today, medicine is widely thought of as a scientific field, but in the past, it was something that involved religion and superstition more than rational thought. The very first doctors and healers were often shamans and priests, and they saw disease as the result of a disruption in spiritual, as well as physical well-being. With the advent of increasingly scientific healing methods in the eighteenth century however, illness became something that was addressed solely on the physical plane. There is much to be said about modern methods of healing. Modern medicine has drastically lowered mortality rates all over the world and brought a better quality of life for most people. Diseases that used to be fatal can now be cured with a simple round of drugs or therapy. However, even modern medicine can find itself baffled with seemingly simple, albeit chronic problems like overweight, depression, or unexplained aches and pains in an otherwise healthy individual. In cases like this, it is sometimes advisable for a patient to seek a holistic health practitioner rather than a*

*regular doctor. Holistic methods can sometimes improve a patient's condition when conventional medicine cannot make a clear diagnosis or establish effective treatment due their more inclusive approach. Here are three of the principles that govern holistic medicine: [1]. A patient has the power to heal himself. Too often, with Western medicine the cure is as bad as the disease. With chemotherapy for instance, healthy cells are killed along with cancerous ones and the patient ends up weaker and sicker than he was in the beginning. Actually, it is a better idea to work with the person's immune system rather than suppress it to favour the action of drugs. A patient should also be advised to take an active role in his healing through the right diet, exercise, and a positive attitude. Aside from that, holistic health promotes positive disposition. If one is so stressed about his or her sickness, chances are, he or she will get weaker. [2]. The root cause must be found and addressed. Conventional medicine often treats the symptoms, not the disease. In the case of insomnia for instance, it is not enough to prescribe sleeping pills. A patient should also learn to relax, manage his stress, and fix any physiological problems that get in the way of a good night's sleep. In this case, the patient does not necessarily need medicines but is taught on how to deal with his or her stressors. For instance, if the insomnia is caused by work, he or she is taught how to organise his or her work pattern as well as schedule. [3]. The goal is to heal the patient, not to kill the disease. Instead of zeroing in on a disease, the goal should be a better quality of life for the patient. This means looking at the patient as a whole person rather than simply resorting to surgery or drugs to prevent the symptoms of a disease from recurring*

## CHAPTER TWELVE

***[12]-Picking a Holistic Health Provider*** *In the modern era, people have become very conscious about their health. In fact, it is a bit ironic that they worry so much about being healthy that they often become sick in their pursuit of the perfect body. This is largely due to a mistaken attitude about the body. Because doctors often target a disease by curing symptoms rather than taking a person's general mental and physical health into account, people adopt a similar attitude when it comes to their bodies. Often, activities meant to keep the body fit such as dieting and working out result in nutritional deficiencies, strain, and stress. That is why it is often advisable to visit a holistic health practitioner aside from your regular doctor. The holistic approach can be very helpful not just in treating certain complaints, but in helping you to keep your body and mind in optimum condition. There are a lot of therapists and health professionals out there, and some are more skilled than others are. The following tips will help you choose the holistic health practitioner who can be of the most assistance to you. [1]. Ask for*

*a referral. Just as it is with any other doctor, it is a good idea to ask a friend or a colleague if they know of any therapist that they can recommend. If they had a good experience with a therapist, then chances are better that you will get good treatment as well. A referral may also help you do a background check and put you more at ease. [2]. Check credentials. Even therapists who practice alternative or complementary medicine should have the right and proper training. Not everyone can legally set themselves up as healers or prescribe treatments and therapies. Make sure that whoever you are seeing has the appropriate certification and licence to practice. Check to see if they have any affiliations to professional organisations or hospitals in your area. You can ask them directly if you want to just as so you would be clear about this. If they are really legitimate, they would not hesitate to show you their licence and credentials. Just tell them that you just want to be sure as there are a lot of people who claim to have undergone healthcare training. [3]. Pay attention to what he is asking. At your initial meeting with your therapist, you will often be asked about your medical history. Expect this interview to take some time, as your history is critical to the treatment that you will be prescribed with. Check whether the therapist is asking relevant questions, including some about your exercise habits, nutrition, sleep patterns, and even the relationships in your life. All of these will have bearing on your health and the approach that will be used with you. On the other hand, if things are not clear to you, do not hesitate to ask. This way, before you proceed in doing any treatment, you know what to expect. [4]. Go with your gut feel. Your instincts will warn you if you're with a disreputable person. But if you feel comfortable and find the health practitioner open-minded, frank and honest, then you're probably in good hands.*

# CHAPTER THIRTEEN

***[13]-Infertility Remedies- Cure Through Vitamins and Minerals?*** *You have a variety of infertility remedies to choose from, from herbs and hormone treatments to artificial methods like IVF and newer medical methods to vitamins and minerals. Yes, you heard that right. Vitamins and minerals are also regarded as infertility remedies for they play a certain role in conception. In this article I will concentrate on infertility remedies like minerals and vitamins. Selenium Male infertility is often caused by a lack of selenium as found out through medical research conducted by the Italian university of Padua. Sperm cell oxidation is prevented through the intake of selenium and when you consume a diet rich in selenium, you can easily maintain the integrity of the sperm cell. You can consume seafood, fish, liver and red meat which are all good sources of selenium. Just make sure the fish is low mercury and the liver organic. To improve low levels you may take multivitamin and mineral tablets which contain both selenium and zinc. Look for one that contains 100 micrograms of selenium and 25*

*milligrams of zinc. A rich and varied diet consisting of fresh fruits, veggies, lean meat, lean protein and dairy products, should give you good amounts of zinc, selenium, vitamins C and E. Zinc Another essential for male and female infertility is zinc that is involved with 200 plus enzymes and proteins. Zinc can activate key sperm enzymes and can move inside the prostate if the testosterone helps it. Testosterone levels are lowered, testicle size is reduced and the sperm that is produced is unhealthy and misshapen when there is a lack of zinc in your diet. In women zinc is necessary for your body to efficiently use the reproductive hormones oestrogen and progesterone. Lack of zinc in women can cause miscarriage. These are only some of the negatives. Hair mineral analysis through a reputable lab is a good way of finding out if you have low zinc or selenium levels. Vitamin E This one is usually taken as a beauty enhancing tablet, but lack of vitamin E can cause loss of fertility in males through lack of sperm production and motility. Some studies suggest its antioxidant activity may make the sperm more fertile. Vitamin E is thought to contribute to fertility in females although there is not a lot of direct evidence to back it up. Therefore to eliminate all these problems and also to eliminate menstrual cramps and pain, you should take 400 IU of vitamin E every day. Among infertility remedies is also Vitamin C, another antioxidant, found in citrus fruits and veggies.*

# CHAPTER FOURTEEN

***[14]-Acupuncture As a InfertilityTreatment***

*Some women have thought that acupuncture can help with infertility by restoring ovarian function. By inserting needles into the skin at certain points, it can stimulate body functions. Although this has not been proven effective by modern medical standards, it has been used throughout Asia for several thousand years. Studies have suggested that acupuncture improves ovulation, therefore increasing the odds of becoming pregnant. Acupuncture has been used in China for the treatment of infertility for centuries. The Chinese break it down to five basic organs- the liver, spleen, heart, lung, and kidney. They use acupuncture to release blockage to allow energy to flow more freely. This enables the body to be restored to overall good health. Therefore it is sufficient to say that it can increase your chances to obtain fertility. Applying acupuncture to the kidney points releases psychological blocks that can interfere with reproduction. Being that there are many reasons why someone can be infertile, the Chinese feel that treating all organs for different reasons can be quite effective. For example, if a person has deep rooted fears, possibly connected to low self-esteem or sexual abuse, they would treat the heart and kidneys. Perhaps a patient is questioning whether or not a psychological issue is involved in the infertility, and not sure what the issue is, they would target the same, just in a different area. They can also address the conception vessel, which is located between the breasts. This is a very important place for women because it opens their energy. The Chinese believe women's menstrual problems would definitely be considered to be connected to their infertility. In order for conception to take place, the womb needs sufficient blood and energy. Acupuncture can help with both the physical body and the emotions. If you're having chills, this could be from poor circulation in general. Regulating your monthly cycle and the activation of blood flow by acupuncture in combination with nourishing herbs could give you the results you're looking for. In regard to your organs, infertility frequently stems from the liver, spleen and kidney. The liver stores blood, the spleen manufactures blood, and the kidney oversees the whole process of reproduction. There are two non-organ elements that play a part with menstruation and infertility. One being the conception vessel, which manages conception, as it's named. This requires blood and energy. The other is the penetrating vessel. This takes blood from the liver to form a reservoir that supplies the conception vessel. Acupuncture can help with male sexual problems as well. Impotence comes from a lack of energy associated with the kidney. The anxiety in your mind can take a toll and can harm the kidney. Following the weakening of the heart, liver, and spleen. These organs are of importance for sexual functions, since they influence blood circulation. Having trouble with them is shown by symptoms of depression, dizziness, worry, nausea and insomnia. There are natural ways to increase your chances of fertility with acupuncture. Having normal kidney function, acupuncture has proven effective in correcting impotence. The lower abdomen is stimulated, which brings forth the energy to assist performance. Sometimes treatment to motivate the liver and other deficiencies is helpful to improve the flow of blood.*

# CHAPTER FIFTEEN

***[15]-Acupuncture : A Different Type Of Treatment*** *Starting a family is an exciting adventure for a couple who wishes to become parents. When you have reached the point where having a baby is what you want, it can be devastating when becoming pregnant does not happen easily. After months of trying with no luck, you may find yourself feeling hopeless and defeated. It is extremely devastating when you have been diagnosed as being infertile. After the decision to have a baby many joys are dreamed of and learning that you will face difficulties getting pregnant is a hard concept to adjust to for both you and your partner. There is hope for couples experiencing infertility, and we are lucky enough to live in an age with many options and treatments including acupuncture for infertility. Acupuncture for Infertility Without Medical Intervention Before meeting with medical doctors, some couples prefer to try a more holistic approach working with different alternative therapies such as acupuncture for infertility. Acupuncture comes from what we consider to be ancient China and is the*

*treatment of disease by using needles strategically placed to open certain energy channels in the body. Acupuncture is used to address many ailments of the human body such as anxiety, weight loss, chronic pain and other issues. When you receive acupuncture for infertility, it is not exactly a targeted treatment. Along with treatment for the reproductive issues, the acupuncturist treats the whole body for balance. There are studies that show a success rate of becoming pregnant after acupuncture for infertility without ever using medical assistance. An example of an infertility drug that contains many side effects, such as multiple births, is Clomid. When a woman receives acupuncture for infertility, the alternative treatment has shown to stimulate egg production with the same levels of success for pregnancy as Clomid. The statistics that are shown for acupuncture for infertility should be enough to persuade you to try it even if you fully plan on trying other medical routes. Acupuncture for Infertility With The Aid Of Medical Resources After you receive a diagnosis that declares you have an infertility problem you will most likely be sent to see a reproductive endocrinologist. It is beneficial for a woman with infertility issues to attend acupuncture for infertility sessions alongside scheduling and attending regular medical exams. At worst, the holistic approach cannot hurt; studies show it can help both the mental and physical health of a woman. There are published studies and various writings on combining a modern medicine approach with various holistic treatments. Women treated with both IVF and acupuncture for infertility have a higher rate of becoming pregnant than women treated only with IVF. Many well known and highly touted infertility centres now have office space devoted to an acupuncturist so they can combine techniques and their expertise. Approaches for Infertile Couples However you choose to approach dealing with an infertility problem, whether you try acupuncture for infertility or something else, it is important to keep in mind that it will be emotionally stressful and will affect your relationship. As a couple, you need to work together to see the light at the end of the tunnel. Therapy as a couple or on an individual basis is a common way to stay emotionally healthy during this period of significant stress. Gestational surrogate, donor eggs, donor sperm and adoption are a few other options even the most infertile couples can take to successfully become parents. To choose the best next step for you and your partner, be sure to speak with an endocrinologist. Being diagnosed with infertility can be heartbreaking. Before rushing into using any medication or having surgery you might want to consider acupuncture for infertility*

## CHAPTER SIXTEEN

***[16]-Treatment For Your Fertility Problems***

*Infertility diagnosis is a difficult issue to digest. Most couples find it rather difficult to accept the findings in the first few weeks after the diagnosis. It is a condition that affects both men and women and is defined as the inability to conceive after six months to one year of unprotected and regular intercourse. It may also be the woman's inability to carry a baby to a full term and resulting in miscarriage. A series of causes have been identified as to largely contribute to fertility issues for both partners. These factors include a woman's age, menstrual cycle, ovulation disruption; a man's sperm count and quality, erectile dysfunction, sexually transmitted diseases and tubal blockages; and environmental and lifestyle factors like excessive alcohol and drug intake and stress. ACUPUNCTURE as INFERTILITY TREATMENT Acupuncture is an age-old process that is proven to alleviate pain and suffering and promote well-being through the use of small, thin needles. These needles are inserted onto pressure points called "acupoints." This age-old Chinese traditional medicine started thousands of years ago and was slowly integrated into the western medical practises. Acupuncture is said to be based on the principles of "vital energy" and balance and harmony of both mind and body. It aims to restore the body's natural balance. It brings renewed energy and revitalised hormones to encourage an overall health makeover. The practice of acupuncture is to aid our bodies heal naturally through new-found energy. Couples who are undergoing IVFs and other artificial reproductive techniques are encouraged to practice acupuncture. Recent studies have found that acupuncture has aided the treatments and has increased the couples' chances to conceive, by helping the body recover its energy balance. It also helps the body regulate hormones and systems and encourages proper blood flow to different organs. It is recommended that women who undergo IVF treatments should practice acupuncture at least half an hour before the scheduled IVF procedure, and half an hour after the embryo transfer. This is explained by the body's natural reaction to the acupuncture session, as the body achieves a higher state of relaxation, in turn relaxing the uterus and making it susceptible to embryo growth and conception. IS ACUPUNCTURE FOR YOU and YOUR PARTNER? Discuss with your partner the possibility of venturing into the acupuncture process and bring the interest to your fertility expert as well. Your physician would want to know this information so as he/ she could adjust treatments for you to better complement your alternative therapy. Acupuncture is known to be a safe procedure with no published side effects and contra-indications. It will definitely help you relax before and after alternative reproductive techniques and maximise your chances of conception. When you decide to try out acupuncture, make sure you find a licensed acupuncturist to perform the procedure. This will assure you the safety of the procedure, as only a licensed acupuncturist knows the exact locations of median points. They also use sterile needles that would ensure that no complications and infections arise. Read more about the benefits of acupuncture and discover them for yourself when you finally decide to try it out. Who knows, the conception you've always been waiting for may just be around the corner, after a few sessions or so.*

## CHAPTER SEVENTEEN

***[17]-Why Many Doctors Endorse Acupuncture*** *The good news for all who have been diagnosed with infertility problems is that there are few methods available that can assist in treating the problem. In spite of the fact that we live in a technologically advanced world, and the IVF success rates are growing, science does not complete the fertility treatment picture. That is not to say that IVF is not effective, as it certainly is, and has helped many couples have a child. You would be surprised to know that many couples are turning their backs on technology for infertility problems. Many are turning to acupuncture for infertility - an ancient Chinese art that has helped many women become mothers. So what exactly is acupuncture? It is a therapy during which very thin needles are inserted under the skin at specific points on the body. The needles have to be inserted exactly at those points and only a skilled acupuncturist can locate those points in your body and stimulate them effectively. The needles regulate specific body functions and can control various physical problems. Like the saying goes, "old is gold"*

*and similarly, this treatment seems to carry its reputation on and on in the medical field. Acupuncture is gaining popularity when compared to other fertility treatments as it has proven to be more beneficial. Research has shown that acupuncture has increased the rate of pregnancy in women who undergo in vitro fertilisation (IVF). These findings are well-supported by a study done in 2002 on 150 women undergoing IVF. Thirty-six women out of 75 who received acupuncture got pregnant. This is a success rate of 48.0%! Similarly, a study of 75 women who received IVF treatment without acupuncture, had a success rate of only 25%. Only 19 women became pregnant. As you can see from the above information, acupuncture can be effective in treating infertility. Let's go on to the main area of discussion and find out how exactly acupuncture treats infertility. It has been used for many infertility problems successfully. It is used in conjunction with herbs to reduce follicle stimulating hormone (FSH) and polycystic ovarian syndrome (PCOS). In conjunction with IVF, acupuncture is done simultaneously with intrauterine insemination or embryo transfer and this can increase the chances of success. Normally, a series of acupuncture treatments would be done a few months before the first procedure. It will also be continued for three months after the pregnancy begins to protect the fetus during that time when the risk of miscarriage is greatest. If you are considering* *acupuncture treatments along with IVF, then it is reasonable to consider whether the additional costs are warranted. IVF costs add up to almost $10,000 per cycle. If you are above 35, then you may need three to five cycles of IVF treatment. Compared to acupuncture for infertility treatment, it is quite expensive. Acupuncture treatment costs around $1,000 per cycle and it could be an investment that can save you a lot of money. I can't recommend a better treatment which has both a high success rate and low cost. So if you want to have acupuncture as your first treatment, it is important to find a good practitioner who is known to your doctor. It is also worth making sure that you are fully covered for acupuncture by your insurance policy. Although insurance for infertility is another part of the story we will not be covering here but if you want to know more on how acupuncture helps in infertility treatment. A lot of people have benefited from it and you certainly don't want to miss out. Go ahead and start your own family with it.*

# CHAPTER EIGHTEEN

***[18]-Benefits and Risks of Using Acupuncture for Infertility*** *Acupuncture originated in the East and has existed for a very long time. It is the technique of applying and adjusting fine needles into specific points on the body to relieve pain and also to treat several medical conditions. Acupuncture usually adjusts blood pressure by stimulating the real central nervous system. It releases endorphins which in turn inhibits pain and offers the body the feeling of wellbeing and also secretes neurotransmitters and neurohormones, which helps the body to recover itself. Acupuncture can be used in conjunction with infertility treatments to cure problems similar to hormonal imbalances. Since it adjusts the body's system, blood flow is enhanced to the vital organs in addition the hormonal levels happen to be effectively regulated. It also boosts follicular and ovarian function. It can increase the blood flow towards the endometrium, assisting to help a rich lining. Acupuncture and IVF Additionally, acupuncture could enhance the effectiveness of IVF or In Vitro Fertilisation. A lot more*

*fertility professionals along with centres offer it as part of their IVF treatment plans. By using acupuncture, the embryo transfer process in IVF was shown to have many improvements leading in many cases to pregnancy. Acupuncture could also be used to cure fertility problems like spasmed tubes. Even though blocked tubes will not likely be affected by acupuncture, sometimes spasmed tubes tend to be de-spasmed by using acupuncture. It is often combined with herbal treatments to cure more FSH or Follicle Stimulating Hormone recurrent pregnancy loss, unexplained (idiopathic) infertility, hyperprolactinemia, and also luteal phase defect, (when not the result of a prolactinoma), PCOSor PolycysticOvarian Syndrome along with irregular menstrual cycles, and also men's factor like men affected with sperm-DNA-fragmentation. Like physical therapy, acupuncture is a procedure that assists the body to cure itself over time. It is actually preferable to use more than less. When Acupuncture treatment is recommended [1]. Women can usually be treated for 3 to 4 months just before an insemination, donor-egg transfer and IVF or in vitro fertilisation. [2]..Women are also recommended to use acupuncture, before and after an embryo transfer. [3].To apply acupuncture for 3 to 4 months before a fertility treatment seems to also have a healing result. [4]. Going via fertility treatments can be very stressful for the couple and for the woman especially.*

*Acupuncture is a great method to decrease stress, anxiousness as well as depression. With so many ways in which acupuncture has a beneficial influence on infertility treatments, it feels right for any couple who is struggling with infertility to test each and every alternative out there. What are the risks of applying the acupuncture for infertility There are almost no dangers when applying acupuncture along with infertility treatments. The most significant risk is the fact that a miscarriage may occur if wrong acupuncture points are utilised if a woman is currently pregnant. That is why employing an acupuncturist who seems to be specialised in the treatment of fertility problems is very important for many who wish to include acupuncture as part of their therapy regimen. Also electro-acupuncture is an excellent replacement for traditional medical pain relievers while in labour. It may also result in quicker hospitalisation times which in turn lead to lower expenses. Plus, research suggests that the most reliable fertility treatment options require combining acupuncture, herbal medicine, as well as traditional medical treatments. Although, acupuncture and herbal medicines won't help conceiving on their own if traditional medical interventions are not used.*

# CHAPTER NINETEEN

***[19]-Where To Obtain Acupuncture For Infertility*** *A recent study found that when in vitro fertilisation as a treatment for infertility, acupuncture and infertility combined improves the success rate by as much as 50%. So what does acupuncture and fertility have to do with each other? If you have read about or studied acupuncture, you know that acupuncture is intended to remove any blockages in the body and restore the flow of Qi, the vital energy of the body. Traditional Chinese acupuncturists treat the whole body, and so the concept is that when the body is in balance through acupuncture, the I.V.F process is more readily accepted. But you don't necessarily have to believe in alternative or Eastern medicine in order to reap the benefits of acupuncture and infertility. There have been many studies done that have shown the therapeutic effects of acupuncture on the human body. Relaxation techniques frequently use acupuncture as a treatment. And many people believe you will not get pregnant if you are not relaxed. If you want to take advantage of this three thousand year old traditional Chinese medicinal*

*technique to help in your infertility problems, or learn how acupuncture and infertility are related, you have a number of options. There are now many fertility clinics that now offer acupuncture treatments as part of their overall infertility treatments. In addition, there are designated acupuncture infertility centres. And finally, you may simply contact a certified acupuncturist and s/he will explain to you how s/he uses acupuncture to treat infertility. You may want to consult with an acupuncturist who has had experience using acupuncture in conjunction with infertility treatments. It is important that you put yourself in the hands of a professional, trained and reliable acupuncturist. There are a number of organisations that offer training and accreditation for acupuncturists. So in order to be as safe as possible, you should refer to one of them when choosing your acupuncturist. If they are accredited, you can be sure they have met the proper training requirements. Most of these organisations also have a list showing practitioners who are under investigation and should therefore be avoided. If you contact any or a few of these organisations, you will be sure to locate a centre that is convenient for you, and where you can learn more about acupuncture and infertility: ➢ Accreditation Commission for Acupuncture and Oriental Medicine (acaom.org) ➢ American Association of Acupuncture and Oriental*

*Medicine (adomonline.org) ➢ American Organisation for Bodywork Therapies of Asia (aobta.org) ➢ Council of Colleges of Acupuncture and Oriental Medicine (ccaom.org) ➢ Federation of Acupuncture and Oriental Medicine Regulatory Agencies (faomra.com)*

# CHAPTER TWENTY

***[20]- Acupuncture - Give it a Try***

*Acupuncture for infertility is a variant that works by stabilising the energy that runs along meridians all over the body. By inserting specially made needles into certain areas of the body, the energy that flows all the length of these meridians are regulated. It is believed that whatever unevenness in the flow of energy around the body may cause all sorts of illnesses like infertility. Acupuncture has fourteen channels and out of it, there are twelve main channels namely: the heart, lung, liver, small intestine, large intestine, stomach, gallbladder, kidney, bladder, pericardium, spleen, and the san jiao. Acupuncture for infertility is more on equalising energy in "qi" across the meridians along with the 3 Yin and Yang channels located on each limb. With an unbalanced flow of energy all over your body, fertility cannot be at its best. Acupuncture can solve these imbalances and in turn cure infertility plus other health problems you might be having. There are many women who suffer from infertility and for various reasons they are incapable of generating even a single egg. For these women, acupuncture for infertility treatment is highly advised. It enhances the flow of energy throughout the body thereby stimulating the production of eggs. Various studies have revealed that acupuncture has a quantifiable end result on decreasing pain and that proves to be one of the accepted cures for pain which means it can also be given by doctors. Acupuncture is not only for pain relief it can be used for almost all kinds of health related problems. Acupuncture for infertility on the other hand will allow the energy flowing properly throughout the channels which can restore the body's health that will be the foundation to start a pregnancy. A lot of women do not mind their health until such time it becomes an obstacle in getting something they want, such as a baby. Taking care of your well-being will ensure your chances of conceiving without any difficulty and it will also guarantee a healthy baby. Acupuncture for infertility is a great way to restore your health that can be used prior to, and all the way during pregnancy to make your child bearing time as comfortable as possible. Acupuncture for infertility injects a new energy into the complicated and unbalanced processes of the human body. It removes obstacles along the channels and stimulates energy to flow more easily throughout the body. With the obstacles removed, it also permits toxins to flow out of the body without much difficulty and most of all it promotes a general sense of good health.*

*Finally, does acupuncture work for infertility? Yes it does. Moreover it is also a great means to cure other bodily problems especially when combined with modern medical ways of treatment.*

# CHAPTER TWENTY-ONE

*[21]- **How To Get Pregnant: Guide** At this point in your life you've to think hard about becoming a parent. It's a big challenge to become one but it's also an extremely fulfilling expertise that you simply shouldn't miss. To be able to get pregnant there are some factors that you simply should be aware of that when applied to your lifestyle and your lovemaking will drastically increase your chances to become pregnant. Here are some useful tips on getting pregnant and ways to treasure parenthood:- (1) Prepare Your Physique: You should take the correct minerals and vitamins, this is very important not only for trying to conceive but once conception has occurred then you'll need to prepare yourself to be able to nourish the unborn in the first couple of weeks. There's a lot to be said on this topic. (2) Find out Whenever you Ovulate: You and your partner ought to know all regarding the female ovulation period. It is the most effective time for a sperm to enter and fertilise an egg to produce an offspring. Many couples forget this important part when asking for ideas on getting pregnant from their doctors. Pregnancy*

*needs fertilisation of a female egg and understanding when it is obtainable is crucial to achieve success. (3) Aside from understanding the ovulation period, it's also essential to learn concerning the best sexual position to make use of to achieve maximum chance of pregnancy. All positions and types may be thrilling and pleasurable but you will find particular ones that lessen the chance of depositing sperm within the cervix like the lady on top position which can result in leakage of sperm. (4) Best Time To Get Pregnant: Know when to bring about love. Discover about how sperm can turn out to be much more or much less active. Plan it to ensure that you make love just as you ovulate with the top quality sperm. Female orgasms can also assist in conception if timed nicely. Knowing the best time to get pregnant is equally important. (5) One of the most important solution on getting pregnant is to be active sexually and have regular intercourse. It's the jump off point to conceiving and also you ought to have fun and take pleasure in performing it. For couples within the prime age for pregnancy, doing it regularly can result in pregnancy within six months as much as a year. But for older and much more mature individuals, it might take longer. (6) Fertility problems are not only a women' concern for women but men as well. Therefore it's important to test sperm production and analyse its quality. It is one of the basic pieces of advice on obtaining a pregnancy. Male sperm production gets decreased by unhealthy habits like smoking, drinking and obesity. You will also find certain conditions that affect male reproductive organs like varicocele which causes the scrotum to warm up and kills sperm cells. Getting help and treatment for these conditions is important to reverse infertility. (7) Whenever you encounter trouble getting pregnant after much more than a year of attempting, you should consult medical doctors and figure out whether you have fertility issues. It might seem scary to complete but it's perfectly normal. Actually, it's extremely recommended to have medical tests done each and every year not just for pregnancy but for the general well being as well. (8) But probably the most essential factor in getting pregnant is not to sense the pressure to be successful. Yes, it's significant to have kids but you don't have to push yourself to do extreme things just to get it done. At times it just comes along whether or not you've prepared for it or not. The above tips, when used properly can dramatically increase your chances of getting pregnant. I truly hope this book will help you better navigate through the sometimes rough waters you may encounter on your way to your future child's sparkling eyes and open arms. Best wishes Emmanuel*

Printed by Libri Plureos GmbH in Hamburg, Germany